Childcare

Also by Rob Schlegel

Childcare

Rob Schlegel

Four Way Books
Tribeca

Library of Congress Cataloging-in-Publication Data

Names: Schlegel, Rob, author.
Title: Childcare / Rob Schlegel.
Description: New York : Four Way Books, [2023]
Identifiers: LCCN 2022033081 (print) | LCCN 2022033082 (ebook) |
ISBN 9781954245563 (paperback) | ISBN 9781954245570 (epub)
Subjects: LCGFT: Poetry.
Classification: LCC PS3619.C424 C48 2023 (print) | LCC PS3619.C424
(ebook) | DDC 811/.6--dc23/eng/20220715
LC record available at https://lccn.loc.gov/2022033081
LC ebook record available at https://lccn.loc.gov/2022033082

This book is manufactured in the United States of America and printed on
acid-free paper.

Four Way Books is a not-for-profit literary press. We are grateful for the assistance
we receive from individual donors, public arts agencies, and private foundations.

This publication is made possible with public funds from the
New York State Council on the Arts, a state agency.

We are a proud member of the Community of Literary Magazines and Presses.

CONTENTS

Miracle of the children   the brilliant
Children   the word
Liquid as woodlands

   —GEORGE OPPEN

THE SENTENCE

In the gospel according to children
Love is a sentence containing a logic no syntax can trace.
Mom throwing parties just to ruin them,
Dad blaming everyone but himself.
You remember it, don't you,

Riding your bike past the city's edge
Into marshlands you thought were protected.
Deep in the grass a box labeled PLOT. From that point on
Did you want them to acknowledge you,
Or leave you alone with your paper boats
Inspired by birds so tired of performing—

♦

Wind buffets the mylar balloon trapped
In the neighbor's red maple.

Am I closer to the sentence than I am to Kisha?

My daughter asks why elk pee on themselves.
They found a logic, I say. Like Nero,
My son says. To light his parties
He burned his own people as lanterns.

◆

My daughter dreamed I used the vacuum hose
To suck the sentence from my eye.

In my notebook I write: the female figure
My father sculpted
Props up a succulent too large for its pot.

Daddy, my daughter says,
When are you going to stop?

◆

She's building a spaceship large enough to carry her
And her toy horse to a planet
Immune to the sentence. My son warns
Of nebulae. What's that, she says.

From earth it looks like a bright patch in the night sky.
But what's it look like from space?

My son turns away. My daughter closes the hatch
Over the horse's head. Stay safe, she says.

◆

Take a sentence of a dozen words. Take
Twelve men and tell to each
One word. Stand the men in a row . . .

Let each think of their word
As intently as they will; nowhere will there be
A consciousness of the whole sentence.

◆

My daughter and I eat lunch at the kitchen table.
My son reads in his room, Kisha is on campus.
The semester has just ended—not even
The radio is playing.

How do you hold mom's hand? my daughter says.
Like this? Our fingers interlace.

Or like this—

POETRY

Is pointless, my son says. If you write that down
I'll kill you. I fear he fears
The attention I give it. I used to drive
Till he fell asleep. Ten minutes, then silence

The river knit with ice. In tonight's movie
A boat swerves against bullets.
He sings the movie's theme. *I kill you,*
You kill me. Plot against all

That is good. Good for whom?
I know every word that rhymes
With my assailant's first name. It's difficult
To achieve real-world fear

In a movie. My son crawls into bed.
There's nothing I need more than you, I say.
Not true, he says. The rudder turns
In my throat. Every sleep he needs me less.

SUBJECTIVE UNITS OF DISTRESS

I

My son loads a toothbrush
With ozone. Tell me what you feel, I say.
I feel like you're a jerk.
No, I say. Tell me what you feel.
I feel like you're worthless and I hate you.

II

My father calls. His father is in the ICU.
I don't know what to say. Well,
My father says, I rototilled the garden today—

III

Between teaching and parenting
I somehow find time to notify my therapist
Of a change to my insurance.

IV

What's your mom's mom's mom's
Mom's name?

V

A man at the ATM is trying to deposit
His hand. Where he is

Is earth. He's my father—my dad
The day before the day of my birth.

VI

In the CVS, neon touches my son and I
Pretending to be strangers.

VII

My mother opens the oven

With an oven mitt. Julie gave me this,
She says. How is she, I say.
Dead, she says. I told you that.

VIII

Kisha is awake—
She thought she heard me groaning in my sleep
As if I suffered a violent blow to my face.

IX

My mother would turn on the faucet,
Wet a bar of soap. Her left hand
Held open my mouth.

X

When will I reach the people I love?
I sit where the shade would be
If there were trees.

INHERITANCE

Why can't I love the painting my sister loves?
It's true the painter was an ass, and yet
There's nothing as mysterious as a fact clearly described
Is something he said. Does everyone

Feel cramped? On the subway, people are beautiful
And dead. Even the birds
Share space. I saw where Dan and Callie sleep.
Are they happy? I mean the birds.

◆

In the MET video installation *Death Is Elsewhere,*
Two siblings sing in a meadow
Surrounded by remnants of volcanic eruptions
That triggered a famine that killed
25 percent of the Icelandic population.
I focus on the siblings to avoid eye contact.
It's like the subway between tragedies—
Everyone perfecting their own style of aversion.

◆

Thomas Edison proposed to equip
The Statue of Liberty with a voice that could be heard
At the northern-most tip of the city.
In the cafe, the barista says *Satan's Bomb*
With almond milk for Sydney.
Someone's ringtone announces
That idiot is trying to reach you on your cell phone device.
I search my phone for long-term health effects
Of feeling anonymous.
A man adjusts his face to fit
The camera's frame. Friends in his feed
Eat the flowers off his shirt. Is a person alone
A portrait?

✦

I count the bones in Gerard David's
The Deposition; the gilded age, impinging.
Callie asks if pursuing the exotic
Is inherently masculine. We're caught off-guard
By a masked man in a red leotard.
It's Ed! he says. When we don't understand
He removes the mask. Ed, from Seaview!
He shows us a picture of his girlfriend in bed—

Hundreds of twenties fanned out in both hands—
And that, Ed says, is eight grand—her inheritance.
We had sex on that money!

                        ◆

Dan says we all have inner lives
But not everyone is granted access.
Callie disagrees, citing "Directive." My sister says
We're in a poem she read.

                        ◆

I stare at the painting of a galloping horse.
The rider, tragic. Is he waving
To the orchardist come to prune
The good-tasting apple tree, or me—
That I might set him free?
Years ago, on my lunch break
At Jimmy John's, I realized the man to whom
I tried selling a book would purchase the book
On Amazon. I push the rider off his horse.
The horse is free. Rider, where shall I

Bury thee? The rolling hills of Pomeroy
Bring the locals local joy.

◆

What do you do when your friends leave
And you're alone with every object in the room?
Mom texts a picture of my daughter's
Stuffed owl. *Should this live here?*
What's worse? Uniformed children, or betraying
Friends and family by writing about them?

◆

Mom says she's only as happy
As her unhappiest child: my sister,
My sister and I. No one's interested in workshopping
The painting. I make another sentence,
Over-spell orchid. Are all my relationships
Predicated on man's obsessive naming?
The painting is called *Inheritance.*

SOUND EVOLVES THE EAR TO HEAR ITSELF

Kisha says I was late to appreciate Lou Reed
Because I was raised in a one-stoplight town
Surrounded by forest and corn. For fun
I sat in my room, Sharpied the cover of *Nevermind*.
But is it true, I say, that Reed's parents
Approved electroshock therapy?

                    ✦

Penelope abandoned Pan at birth.
She thought he was ugly. My son says
Pan had this cool ability called
Panic—when he yelled, everything around him
Ran away.

                    ✦

I stress-eat chips in the kitchen
Listening to Audie Cornish
Narrate Kavanaugh, which is totally abstract
Till my son asks me about it.

                    ✦

Pitys escaped Pan by transforming
Into a tree from which Pan tore a branch
He wore as a garland to chase Syrinx to the river.
To avoid Pan, Syrinx became a reed.

◆

Pan's not gone. Merely replaced
By a more cunning god.

◆

The morning after his sleepover
My son's in bed with his friend. I spin in my chair—
Yet half a beast is the great god Pan,
To laugh as he sits by the river,
Making a poet out of a man:
The true gods sigh for the cost and pain . . .

◆

My first panic attack was three months
Into ignoring my desire for a man.
What was it my parents warned?

Just living is difficult enough
Even for people who are normal, like us.

◆

Was every note Pan played played in vain?
Some animals are afraid
Long after the cause of their fear is gone.
Are they hungry?

◆

Here I should record a joy. At a party
Kisha said when you forgive yourself
You become the music you love.
Dance, she said, surrender your body to song.
The DJ played *Kill Your Sons*.

PALE EVENING DUN

The sculptor points to her favorite mayfly—
Yellow abdomen the length of my nail, wings
Like translucent sails—it was alive
For a day. She'd pinned hundreds
To foam-core boards. We correspond
In lengths of twine; a secret code
She insists is improving her art.
Mostly, it's confusing, especially at first,
Back when the insects her collection didn't exist

And I hadn't experienced the competing
Sorrows of parenthood. What can I do
To ensure that my children are just? I say.
The sculptor suggests I've gone too long
Without being moved by the surprise shape
Of a non-human sentient being.

Two months later I receive from her estate
A framed display of a dozen mayflies.
That night I describe the video to my son.
And that, I say, is why we protest.
Not all police are bad, he says—

The screen door slams. It's responsible of you
To talk to him, Kisha says, but next time
Make a plan. I wear a mask
To pick up my son's equations. His teacher
Hands me a seedling. Sweet
Basil. He should rub these leaves between his fingers
And smell them, she says. Tell him
I miss him. She looks exhausted

Like she might be married to a poet using news.
On my way home I stop beside a stream.
A mayfly lands on my knee. My first impulse
Is to capture it, show it to my son.
I show him two headlines. One is a lie.

LUCID RUSE

The baby shits the bed again. Little herring,
Let's bathe, you and me.

I'll tell you a ghost story—

Housesitting for Joshua
For Emma, Forever Ago on repeat for hours
Asleep on the couch
I felt hover a ghost—
Go find Brandon, I said
Place your icy fingers around his shingled ribs—
In the morning I emptied a bottle
Of Garnier Fructis Fortifying shampoo.
Is Joshua's hair curlier than mine?
Must be. He's your standard
Tropical bird type—books arranged
By subject on tables in every room.
I wrote to Joshua: I love your apartment's
Friendly ghost . . .

After cleaning the sheets
Me and the baby are naked on the bed.
What poet hasn't wished at least once in their life
That poetry was dead?

FIVE DREAMS

IT BEGINS PREDICTABLY: a few awkward passes, tentative shots on goal, each team adjusting to the tempo of the other. In the fourth minute the ball rolls out of bounds. My daughter lifts it over her head as if to pass. The ball vanishes. Her teammate shuffles her feet. A third teammate kicks her leg so convincingly that a wave of energy ripples the back of the opponent's net. The entire team conjures movements that seem spontaneous, yet choreographed, suggesting months, if not years of practice. In the second half, opposing players realize their significance in what will soon be called *All that is Particular in its Splendor, Belongs*. I can feel in my left palm where forgiveness begins. As time runs out, a polychromatic haze lingers over the grass. I'm increasingly comfortable imagining myself in a future irreducible to the past.

ME AND BARYSHNIKOV get high and wreck his house. I throw stemware through windows. He stabs a hole into the painting over the mantle. Kreisler's "Liebesfreud" carries us from one room to the next. Gripping the crown molding over the bedroom door Misha executes the perfect pull-up. "What," he says, "I blame for every fuck-ups in my life my parents?" The cast of his shoulder! The angle of his jaw! Even the splay of his fingers! There's more to see in him than any other. He strikes the floor with Pushkin's cane; up springs fresh water. When his wife returns earlier than expected Misha looks ruined over a bowl of antique marbles, a bloody tooth in his lap. I sneak into the tub, hoping the water mellows my crash. I imagine Misha in bed, moving in on his wife, his wife pushing back. Delighted with the night exactly as the night unfolded, I'm just this side of gone, which is to say, inside this body that will deliver me out of sleep and into the garden, where I hope to find Misha waiting at the table white with wine and rose.

I MEET MY SISTER and her friends at Fusion—a rebellious place, prodigal with aromas of jasmine and lemongrass, ginger and mint. Despite her penchant for strong opinions, my sister modulates the volume of her voice better than anyone I know. But I worry she'll reveal the jock in me; I can see myself so clearly, years ago on the mound, afraid almost at the certainty of my desire to be drafted. Over eel cakes my sister says, "How's the poetry?" "I see only defects in what I'm doing," I say, "and the mutability of my sentences! They're sure to become the weakest monuments to my existence." My scalp is hot from the green chilies in the brisket pho. Then my sister's blindside. "You wore number ten! And your out-pitch was a change-up!" The rest of the meal is a steady procession of criticisms punctuated by a burst of dessert flame. My sister's friend changes the tone. "…and aren't we more than just our father's daughters and mother's sons?"

MEMORIAL DAY

My mother slices bread on the patio.
My father just mowed the grass.
I haven't seen them since they watched the kids
When Kisha and I were in Atlanta
For her brother's funeral. More birds
This spring than last, my father says.

My mother leans in her chair, pulls a weed.
I don't touch the bread. In the garden
The asparagus is tall, but sparse.
We inspect the rhubarb. How are the poems,
My father says. Whatever I say
Will feel like a lie. I show them the app

That claims to identify all flora
With 98% accuracy. My father kneels
Over a star-shaped flower.
Siberian Spring Beauty. And that? he says.
Common Elder. According to the app,
"Elder" derives from the Anglo-Saxon "æld,"

Meaning "fire." My mother points.
Is that the poison ivy you used in your sculpture?
Remember that? she says, laughing.

Six hours in the E.R., Christmas Eve,
2003. I prefer thinking over feeling; future
Over past. Back on the patio

My father shows me the book he made.
Each page features a portrait
From life-drawing, December 2019.
The book is called *12 Faces*.
Drive safe, my mother says, when I leave.

THE MAELSTROM

1.

I tuck my son into bed.
I wish I had better parents, he says.

He needs my love the most when he least deserves it
Is something I read.

I make up a story about me and my father
Stranded in a boat a mile offshore.
We wave and yell, but my son's too far away to hear.

I leave when I think he's asleep.
Minutes later he's in my room with a journal.
Can you write in this for me, he says,
But no poetry.

2.

He asks me to say something besides
"Have fun" every time I drop him off at school.
I ask what he prefers. Try not
To die, he says. What was I thinking

The first time I held him?
Reaching for a handful of snow
I accidentally pull an early crocus.
I hate repeating myself. I kiss the crocus,

Offer it to my son. In his hands
It becomes a feather. Winter geese
Move between worlds. Once, I hunted them.
To dress them I used my sharpest blade.

My son says a feather in your pocket
Is good luck. I learn to love the blade
By mourning what it cuts.

3.

After hunting mushrooms
We sleep in the tent I used to sleep in
With my grandfather.

On his deathbed I brushed his hair,
My father applied Vaseline
To his dry lips. In the living room
We stared at the cat.

My grandfather died in the dying-room;
His face a chanterelle
Emerging from duff in the woods.

4.

In the mail, a postcard of a battleship,
Its cannons covered in moss.
November greetings from Brandon.

I crawl inside the cannon.
There's Brandon. I realized something
About your poetics, he says.

What you love about Hopkins
Is his compression and repetition.
Sprung rhythm, I say.

But Hopkins didn't invent that, he says.
Compression and repetition
Is the life of the incarcerated.

5.

In the window my son studies his face.
There are three ways to die, he says.
Asleep. Awake. And somewhere in-between.

There's the sun's flaming edge.
I pull a hook through my palm.
The air folds like a school of fish.

Am I one among the few who believe
We're not supposed to outlive the sea?
I stitch my wound with seaweed
Summer lengthened in a narrative
Whose hero is a villain. Boys push boys

Into waves. Once, on the bus
My friends and I made jokes
About each other's parents. One boy said something
I can't remember now about my father.

At least I have a dad, I said.

6.

I rub saliva on the back of my son's neck
To see the map our forefathers' stitched.
He transforms into a plastic bag filled with air.
There he goes. I reach my hand

Into water. The first fish
Slips through. The second stings.
The third is a book famous for naming.
Its pages lead me to a cave
Filled with men I keep company
Till my son returns, heavy with seawater.

To save him I must puncture him.
But where, and with what sacred object?

7.

I throw the book into water surrounded by trees
In April frost which quiets the house enough
That I can study the flag obscuring
The violence of cutting off the hands
Of the mother and replacing them
With the paws of the lion.
Through a maze of submerged logs

Fish of various size chase nymphs. I know the evil
In men. But the poem delays. Death
Names my shape. I keep my clothes

From dust and ghosts and time.
I'm angry at my father for aging,
For paving roads through mountains
Slowly at first, then faster
Into valleys and straight to the ocean
No human can survive. Will I know the words
That will bring him back to life?

8.

I tuck my son into bed.
How are you? I say.

You have to ask?

He's been reading the news.
The more we learn, I say,
The safer we make ourselves and others.

Or, he says, the more we learn
The scarier things are.
I rub his back. He rolls on his side,
Curls his body against mine.
Into his chest he pulls
My hands. I'm a seahorse held

By a sea. I check-in with my head
Like an old house I'm watching for a friend.
Inside fall many kinds of rain—

My son is a vessel
To carry people between—

I mourn how far we've come.

(UN)CONDITIONAL

If waves where they break

If my son's mouth

If it's mine how I see

If the sentence is a hell help me cross

If conditions are perfect

If the clothes fit

If it's true what they say

If consciousness is crystal

If matter exists

Can you see through it

If my plate is full

If a sink of dirty dishes

If anus is the soul

If *same* is *instead*

If I could spin in this dizzy

If pretend

If selfcare is selfish

If enchanted leather pants

If contemplative

If Kisha gives till she's gone

If my son says fuck off

If he doesn't

If the cut draws blood

If life ends in desire

If it begins in love

ASSISTED LIVING

How are the kids, my father says.
Ready for summer, I say.
Well, he says, your grandmother
Can no longer move on her own.
Every morning two caregivers lift her from bed
And into her chair, then to the toilet,
Back to her chair—

In the background I can hear my mother
Narrate the sun setting over the coast range—

She hits them, my father says. She hurts them
Because she thinks they're hurting her.

Out my window, a man stands in the elm.
He's cutting limbs before they fall
On another car. Only a matter of time, he said,
Before one lands on a person.

My father and I say goodbye
But he forgets to end the call.
I listen to the silence between them.
How many relationships are built around it?

Look at the sunset, now, my father says,
It's just beautiful.

CREEPING THYME

A car rolls to a stop.
Want a lift, the passenger says.
The red leather seats
Are exquisitely clean.

Our road hugs a sea.
The driver's eyes
Drift. By the time we arrive
The passenger sleeps.

The driver and I lock eyes.
C'mere, she says.
When she moves the passenger's head
It comes off in her hands.

Take it, she says.
Inside, my children feed it
A spoonful of sand.
Come, wind. Come, rain—

Carry April into May!
Over the door I secure the head.
It can see both ways.

Have you always been called "Rob"?

Robbie, I say.

Let's try something. See the pillow?
That's Robbie. What's he like?

He doesn't live in fear, I say,
He's mostly just alive.

Can you pick him up, hold him to your chest?
I shut my eyes.

I remember the delivery room, mid-April.
The lilacs obscene. The midwife
Says the baby is breech, hours away—

Oh the fuck it is, Kisha says
Summoning the ocean inside her
Which carries her body through plaintive breaks
Peripheries we come from,
The strange vast ruins in which I believe—

The baby emerges at a weird angle
The midwife anticipates. She receives him beautifully—
But no more so than Kisha delivered him
From one emergency into the next.

Dad? The midwife hands me a pair of scissors.

It's the kind of morning a child
Bleary-eyed from a night of swimming
Might emerge from the house to find her sibling
Face-down in the water—

But my children are merely sleeping
And I can't separate their beauty
From the future violence they will commit,
Nor from the violence to be committed against them.

w

a

s

p

s

enter the nest shaped
like the globe I'd spin, stop with
a finger on the X of my death. I empty
a can of poison. The next day the wrong part
of the nest is melted; wasps cling to the eave
as if consulting with each other on the shape
and meaning of time. My daughter spots
a whale spouting offshore. Days
after swimming in the ocean
I can feel the ocean
at home in my
ear.

The Giant Pacific Octopus weaves her eggs
Into strands she hangs from the ceiling of a cave.
For months she waves her arms,
Providing them a steady supply of fresh water.
She eats nothing. Months

Become years. When they hatch
Her babies are the size of a grain of rice. She blows them
From the cave. Then dies.

In a crack in the neighbor's wall
A spider wraps silk around an inchworm.
My son kicks the wall—
The spider retreats—

What are you doing, I say.
Intervening, he says.

Is the difference between suffering and survival
lost in my refusal to take a side?

But that was yesterday, when who I was
haunts me like the lowercase tragedy
life is.

Outside the curved lines of a cloud
My daughter colors the sky red.
I sit on the floor and count my breaths.
Color with me, she says.

When the minute-hand reaches the ten,
I say. She walks in a circle
Around me. Against my ear she presses
The cool face of my watch.

What would you rather have, I say,
The ability to know what others are feeling,
Or the power to stop time?

She can feel you staring,
My daughter says of the heron
In the pond in her drawing.

I sponge the milk my son spilled.
He dares his sister to read my mind.

Kisha thaws chicken on the counter.
Is it dangerous to defrost
Feelings at room temperature?

In the painting of the ocean over the TV
The illusion of movement
Distilled in waves about to fall
Is all the more vital for being trapped
On paper. *What if*

Is one way to begin. The rose
Tapping the window wants in. I ask my son
If there's a god or goddess of time.

There's only culture, he says.

My daughter can't sleep.
When she closes her eyes she sees herself
Cutting the cat with a knife.

She pretends to be Isaac; I'm Margot.
We build a castle with pillows and books.
Dearest Margot, she says,
What do you ponder?

Contagions. Contract renewal.

Merrill's *Collected Poems*
Reinforces a castle wall. How many angels
Does it keep? How many demons?

Three weeks after burying the bird
The cat left on the porch
My daughter asks what the bird
Looks like now. What if
Everything we say
Is one long sentence that only ends
When we end?

Fine, my daughter says, but what do you mean
End?

Love poem for my son his breath a net
For grief a climate
For my daughter's face cobwebs break
For Kisha awake in the night
For the earth a book burning in water
For my family when I'm not here
For everything I feel
For language when it's ready to heal

What that means I can only fathom in trees

I wonder how they see me

My children know, but will they, when it's time
Sit with me when I

A maze of paths funnel me
Toward a square of glass
In whose reflection I'm two people—
One not speaking to the other—

I build a boat and call it Song.
Its oars transform into the sons of Ares
Who deliver me to an ocean ruled
By the Sorceress of the Palace of Seaweed.

She synchs my pulse to the jellies.
That you long to see, she says,
Suggests your relationship to death is rich—
But water favors those who feel it.

I have no place to put everything
My children make me feel.

Can I imagine a future
In which they reject me—
Cracks in the hull of the vessel we're in—
How far I would swim to save them.

Like waves, they threaten my capacity to love
Then vanish love's limits.

The shore is filled with men
Chanting lyrics to my favorite song.
I pretend to sing, but not until I'm home
Washing my daughter's hair.
The commotion down the hall
Is my son pinning the future against the wall.

My daughter asks how the world ends.
I imagine a shore, quiet, except for the cry of gulls,
The occasional rush of a thin wave—

What's the word for when the water's
Almost raging? One plan is to fall
Into the arms of the person you love.
Another is forgetting. I believe in no god
But the one that lives knee-deep in the waves
When the waves are sharp and stinging.

With their magic the children move us
Around the house. Pretend we know
More than we think, or just enough
To keep moving, naming feelings after blossoms
The wind lifts up and over the street—

I learn to identify the Daphne
Not by the scent of its blossoms
But by its green and pale green leaves
I remember my father raking.

Is that his voice from the open window
Or mine, years from now
When the trees cast twice their current shade
And the waves reach into the lives our children made—

You've read the script. It opens in spring.
This is where we live—the street,
The stars—pretend the poem is made of this.
Pretend it never ends.

The long hand points to the minute,
Short hand the hour.
Where will I be
When you die, my daughter says.

She places a wreath of thyme
In a hole in the trunk of the hawthorn.

There's an easier way, I say.
But I'm too late.

Branches descending like arms
Lift her into the canopy.

From here, she says, I can see.

Birds?
At every grave.

Clouds?
One.

Our prayers?
All wrong.

What is time like?
A green lake.

Can you touch it?
I learn the contradictions.

Do they end?
Who would we be if they did?

Winds?
Warm.

Is there a flag?
Kids wave branches like wands.

What is it called?
May.

JUNE

I hold the line to a kite. When it falls
What remains of the sentiment

That it was flying? Higher, the children say.
I let go more line.

NOTES

Thank you to the editors of: *Bennington Review, The Canary, The Iowa Review, The Nation, Old Pal, Poetry,* and *Poetry Daily,* where some of these poems appeared.

*   *   *

"The Sentence"
The section beginning, "Take a sentence of a dozen words" is indebted to William James's *Principles of Psychology.*

"Inheritance"
"*There's nothing as mysterious as a fact clearly described*" is indebted to Garry Winogrand; "the gilded age, impinging" is indebted to Christian Schlegel.

"Sound Evolves the Ear to Hear Itself"
Italicized lines are from Elizabeth Barrett Browning's "A Musical Instrument." "Here I should record a joy" is indebted to Clarice Lispector.

"Pale Evening Dun"
"Without being moved by the surprise shape / Of a non-human sentient being" is indebted to David Abram's *Becoming Animal: An Earthly Cosmology.*

"Five Dreams"
Section 4 is indebted to *The Journal of Eugène Delacroix.*

"The Maelstrom"
"I keep my clothes // From dust and ghosts and time" is indebted to Paul
Thomas Anderson's *Phantom Thread*.

"Creeping Thyme"
Section 6 is indebted to Maja Säfström.
"I believe in no god / But the one that lives knee-deep in the waves /
When the waves are sharp and stinging" is indebted to Lauren Groff.

*   *   *

Thank you Brian Blanchfield, Alan Felsenthal, Callie Garnett, Jessica
Laser, Mark Leidner, James Longenbach, John Myers, Daniel Poppick,
Kisha Lewellyn Schlegel, and Grayson Wolf for reading earlier versions
of these poems. You have changed my head and heart. Thank you, also,
to Whitman College, the Mineral School, and the Four Way family.

Rob Schlegel lives in the Pacific Northwest. With the poets Rawaan Alkhatib and Daniel Poppick, he co-edits the Catenary Press.

Publication of this book was made possible by grants and donations. We are also grateful to those individuals who participated in our Build a Book Program. They are:

Anonymous (13), Robert Abrams, Michael Ansara, Kathy Aponick, Jean Ball, Sally Ball, Clayre Benzadón, Adrian Blevins, Laurel Blossom, adam bohannon, Betsy Bonner, Patricia Bottomley, Lee Briccetti, Joel Brouwer, Susan Buttenwieser, Anthony Cappo, Paul and Brandy Carlson, Mark Conway, Elinor Cramer, Dan and Karen Clarke, Kwame Dawes, Michael Anna de Armas, John Del Peschio, Brian Komei Dempster, Rosalynde Vas Dias, Patrick Donnelly, Lynn Emanuel, Blas Falconer, Jennifer Franklin, John Gallaher, Reginald Gibbons, Rebecca Kaiser Gibson, Dorothy Tapper Goldman, Julia Guez, Naomi Guttman and Jonathan Mead, Forrest Hamer, Luke Hankins, Yona Harvey, KT Herr, Karen Hildebrand, Carlie Hoffman, Glenna Horton, Thomas and Autumn Howard, Catherine Hoyser, Elizabeth Jackson, Linda Susan Jackson, Jessica Jacobs and Nickole Brown, Lee Jenkins, Elizabeth Kanell, Nancy Kassell, Maeve Kinkead, Victoria Korth, Brett Lauer and Gretchen Scott, Howard Levy, Owen Lewis and Susan Ennis, Margaree Little, Sara London and Dean Albarelli, Tariq Luthun, Myra Malkin, Louise Mathias, Victoria McCoy, Lupe Mendez, Michael and Nancy Murphy, Kimberly Nunes, Susan Okie and Walter Weiss, Cathy McArthur Palermo, Veronica Patterson, Jill Pearlman, Marcia and Chris Pelletiere, Sam Perkins, Susan Peters and Morgan Driscoll, Maya Pindyck, Megan Pinto, Kevin Prufer, Martha Rhodes, Paula Rhodes, Louise Riemer, Peter and Jill Schireson, Rob Schlegel, Yoana Setzer, Soraya Shalforoosh, Mary Slechta, Diane Souvaine, Barbara Spark, Catherine Stearns, Jacob Strautmann, Yerra Sugarman, Arthur Sze and Carol Moldaw, Marjorie and Lew Tesser, Dorothy Thomas, Rushi Vyas, Martha Webster and Robert Fuentes, Rachel Weintraub and Allston James, Abigail Wender, D. Wolff, and Monica Youn.